Musical Art and Study

Papers for Musicians

Henry C. Banister

CAMBRIDGE UNIVERSITY PRESS

Cambridge, New York, Melbourne, Madrid, Cape Town,
Singapore, São Paolo, Delhi, Tokyo, Mexico City

Published in the United States of America by Cambridge University Press, New York

www.cambridge.org
Information on this title: www.cambridge.org/9781108038560

© in this compilation Cambridge University Press 2011

This edition first published 1887
This digitally printed version 2011

ISBN 978-1-108-03856-0 Paperback

This book reproduces the text of the original edition. The content and language reflect the beliefs, practices and terminology of their time, and have not been updated.

Cambridge University Press wishes to make clear that the book, unless originally published by Cambridge, is not being republished by, in association or collaboration with, or with the endorsement or approval of, the original publisher or its successors in title.

CAMBRIDGE LIBRARY COLLECTION
Books of enduring scholarly value

Music

The systematic academic study of music gave rise to works of description, analysis and criticism, by composers and performers, philosophers and anthropologists, historians and teachers, and by a new kind of scholar - the musicologist. This series makes available a range of significant works encompassing all aspects of the developing discipline.

Musical Art and Study

Henry Charles Banister (1831–97) is best-remembered for *Music*, his textbook on harmony published in 1872 which ran through many editions during his life, and for his biography of the composer Sir George Macfarren. In his capacity as a professor at the Royal Academy of Music and the Guildhall School of Music, a teacher at the Royal Normal College for the Blind, and a member of the National Society of Professional Musicians, he gave many lectures and papers to widely varying audiences. Three of these form this volume, first published in 1887. The first, given to the National Society in 1887, discusses the nature of music as a profession and his thoughts on the difference between the professional and the amateur. The second and third papers consider approaches to the study of the theory and structure of music, its appreciation as an art form and its role in society.

Cambridge University Press has long been a pioneer in the reissuing of out-of-print titles from its own backlist, producing digital reprints of books that are still sought after by scholars and students but could not be reprinted economically using traditional technology. The Cambridge Library Collection extends this activity to a wider range of books which are still of importance to researchers and professionals, either for the source material they contain, or as landmarks in the history of their academic discipline.

Drawing from the world-renowned collections in the Cambridge University Library, and guided by the advice of experts in each subject area, Cambridge University Press is using state-of-the-art scanning machines in its own Printing House to capture the content of each book selected for inclusion. The files are processed to give a consistently clear, crisp image, and the books finished to the high quality standard for which the Press is recognised around the world. The latest print-on-demand technology ensures that the books will remain available indefinitely, and that orders for single or multiple copies can quickly be supplied.

The Cambridge Library Collection will bring back to life books of enduring scholarly value (including out-of-copyright works originally issued by other publishers) across a wide range of disciplines in the humanities and social sciences and in science and technology.

MUSICAL ART AND STUDY

MUSICAL ART AND STUDY

Papers for Musicians

BY

HENRY C. BANISTER

PROFESSOR OF HARMONY AND COMPOSITION AT THE
ROYAL ACADEMY OF MUSIC, THE ROYAL NORMAL COLLEGE AND
ACADEMY OF MUSIC FOR THE BLIND, AND THE
GUILDHALL SCHOOL OF MUSIC

London
GEORGE BELL AND SONS
YORK STREET, COVENT GARDEN
1887

CAMBRIDGE
PRINTED BY JONATHAN PALMER
ALEXANDRA STREET

PREFATORY NOTE.

The third of these Papers has appeared in the Year-book of the College of Organists, but is now first presented to a wider circle of readers. The first Paper, originally read in London, and repeated at Croydon and Brighton, by desire of the Council of the South-Eastern section of the National Society of Professional Musicians, is published in compliance with many requests. The three Papers, although prepared at different times and for different audiences, deal to some extent with cognate subjects; and I have not thought it necessary to eliminate a few repetitions of similar thoughts.

H. C. B.

LONDON, *May* 1887.

CONTENTS.

		PAGE
I.	OUR ART AND OUR PROFESSION	1
II.	SOME METHODS OF MUSICAL STUDY	19
III.	SOME MUSICAL ETHICS AND ANALOGIES	45

I

Our Art and our Profession

[*Read before the National Society of Professional Musicians, February* 12*th*, 1887]

Our Art and our Profession.

I ESTEEM it a high honour that I should be requested by our Council to address you on some aspects of our purpose and work, not of a business character; indeed, on matters which affect us as musical artists and professors, quite irrespective of any membership of this Society. It is of the first importance that we aim high, and realise the dignity of our calling; and therefore I propose to make a few remarks upon *our Art and our Profession*, which shall tend to elevate our thoughts, and lift us out of mere business considerations, such as we are very liable to be credited with; our Society being regarded by some as little more than a somewhat superior—perhaps hardly superior—kind of trades-union. We are a *Society*; that is certainly a *union*. We are a *Professional* Society; and that which we profess is Music, the ethereal *Art.* Our *Art* and our *Profession*, then, are certainly fitting topics for our consideration as a Society. With our *nationality* I do not purpose dealing; save to say that it is not insular, exclusive. Our *Art* is cosmopolitan; and nationality with us means, I take it, the largest approach that we can make towards all-embracing universality. Therefore, our nationality is not a grandiose vaunt; it is an inevitable limitation. You do not need me to urge or

> *To prove again that Music, by the plea*
> *Of all men's love, has link'd from sea to sea*
> *All shores of earth in one serene and grand*
> *Symphonic land.*

Would that, with loftiest purpose, we could reach and influence, and be influenced by, all true musical artists; all lovers of the world-wide—nay, let us rather believe—universe-wide Art. But, with the limitations which we cannot break through, we must simply feel that

> *A joy to the heart is a goal that it may not reach.*

Our Art and our Profession: these are named, not in opposition, but in apposition; not as inconsistent, but as parallel; not with the contrast sometimes implied when profession and practice are mentioned together. Our *Art* is our *Profession*; we profess our *Art*. I read, indeed, that "it is on record that in the year 886 A.D. the king [Alfred] bestowed on one of the teachers of [musical] theory [in Oxford University], by name John, the title of '*Professor of Music,*' which is probably the first appellation of its kind."* The

---

* Naumann's *History of Music*, p. 201.

term, philologically, means, I believe, to speak forth, and would be specially applicable to one who lectured or taught from a chair, *ex cathedrâ*. It would therefore be appropriate rather to a theoretical instructor than to one teaching an instrument. Somehow or other, Music is not reckoned among the *learned professions*. I read in an Encyclopædia that the word "Professor" is now "occasionally used in a loose way. . . . It has been assumed as a designation not only by instructors in music and dancing, but by conjurors."* But we have seen that more than a thousand years ago it was royally conferred on a musical theorist.

I suppose that an impression prevails that it is not a matter of much learning to be a musician, even a theoretical musician. Well, there are certainly the three learned professions: *Divinity*, which should perhaps hardly be so much a profession as an inspiration, and which, at all events, is too often pursued with professional perfunctoriness. But that which we profess has the like heavenly, divine origin; it is not man-made. There is *Law*, with its history, its logic, its entanglements and perplexities. I am not sure but that, while we can exceed it in attractiveness, we can also match it for intricacy, when we deal with double, triple, and quadruple counterpoints, and such matters.

---

* Chambers' *Encyclopædia* s. v. 'Professor.'

4 MUSICAL ART AND STUDY.

And there is *Physic*, which has oft-times been empirical and uncertain, though so beneficent. We may claim some affinity with the healing art. From the days of Saul, king of Israel, Music has not unfrequently "ministered to a mind diseased," whether or not it has "soothed the savage breast." However, learned or not, our *Profession* is our *Art*. Truly, Music has not for its function to add to our learning, to increase our knowledge; although a German thinker says, "The wonderful thing in Music is that it, while appealing entirely to the emotions, does so on one side entirely through the understanding, namely, through the strictest mathematics of tones.* And our great living poet-philosopher says:

> *There is no truer truth obtainable*
> *By man than comes of music . .*
> *. . . . . . to match and mate*
> *Feeling with knowledge,—make as manifest*
> *Soul's work as Mind's work, . . .*
> *. . . . have the plain result to shew*
> *How we feel, hard and fast as what we know—*
> *This were the prize and is the puzzle which*
> *Music essays to solve. . . . .*
> *All Arts endeavour this, and she the most*
> *Attains thereto.†*

But there is another misapplication implied of this term *Professor*, when it is used to distinguish

---

* Rothe, *Still Hours*, p. 367.
† Browning's *Parleyings with Certain People*, pp. 201, 204—5.

the holder of it from an *Amateur*. I claim, and I believe that you, my professional brethren, will join me in the claim, to be the truest *Amateur*. It is by virtue of being a most intense *Amateur* that I am what I am as a *Professor*, if I am in the least worthy of the honourable designation. A *lover* of my Art! A lover of the "heavenly maid" who is ever "young." And, unlike many a so-called *Amateur*, not a lover trifling with the object of my affections: not treating her as a toy to be played with, a pastime; but as a pursuit. It is, with us, not indeed an "inordinate affection, which is idolatry"; but a *cult*, the ideal and type of all that is proportional, pure, beautiful, ethereal.

All the more intelligibly then and emphatically may I now reiterate, if you have gone with me in this sketch of the relations of our *Art* and our *Profession*, that, these relations being intimate, contrast is not implied between the two terms. We must not lightly join in the common talk about *sinking* the *Artist* in the *Professor:* let us rather accept it as our vocation to *absorb* the *Professor* in the *Artist;* to be good professors, because we are true artists. Again I say,—we *profess* our *Art*. We profess, in our several spheres, to understand it; all to love it, and to be under its spell. Some of us, from inevitable circumstances, are more limited in our range than others; only professing to understand, with any approach to completeness, one branch of the art, such as performance on a particular instrument, and the like. And there is something touching in the enthusiasm of any one for the particular branch that he follows; so that it is with a kindly smile that one hears a violinist apostrophise his instrument:

> *Mine Amati—my beloved one—*
> *The tender sprite who soothes, as best he may,*
> *My fever'd pulse, and makes a roundelay*
> *Of all my fears.*
> *When he talks to me, I feel the touch*
> *Of some sweet hope, a feeling of content*
> *Almost akin to what by joy is meant.**

Others, without professing much about it, perhaps, are recognised as *all round* men; *rangé*, more or less compassing the bearings of the various departments of the art, historical, theoretical, æsthetical, and practical. Directly a man wilfully dwarfs his estimate, contracts his range, and estimates his own department out of proportion to the art as a whole, he is losing the artistic and becoming a charlatan; as when a pianoforte player—or, in fact, instrumentalist of any kind—thinks that executive skill is *in itself*, for its own sake, to be exhibited for admiration; or a vocalist, or vocal teacher, regards mode of production as the prime element of excellence; or the theorist measures compositions by their compliance with grammatical *formula*;—

---

* *Love-letters of a Violinist*, pp. 12, 13.

all these things being so excellent *in* themselves, but not *by* themselves; and being, moreover, so possible apart from *Art* in the high sense in which we are using the term. Do we not know those who, under pretence of liberality, non-prejudice, non-pedantry, and the like, profess openness to all styles (of excellence, it is assumed) in our art, but who, with all this, are the very reverse of "all-round" men, or *artists*? A man is a professor, only in the sense of being a pretender, who, under guise of unprejudiced breadth of thought, declares his admiration of certain methods of composition, or of performance, in such manner as to barely disguise, —not, indeed, his *preference* for these, which may be within a truly critical right, though abstractedly wrong; but his half disdain of the older methods, as having had their day, and become effete. As is said with regard to one old master's works—

> *They seem*
> *Dead—do they? lapsed things lost in limbo? Bring*
> *Our life to kindle theirs, and straight each king*
> *Starts, you shall see, stands up, from head to foot*
> *No inch that is not Purcell!**

Such criticism betrays defectiveness both of historical and of philosophical and reflective training, whatever sensibility there may be to beauty. As an acute critic† says:—" Some will have nothing else but what they call pure imagination. Now, air-

---

* Browning's *Parleyings*, p. 213.   † Landor.

plants ought not to fill the whole conservatory; other plants, I would modestly suggest, are worth cultivating, which send their roots pretty deep into the ground. I hate both poetry and wine—[to which we may add music]—without body. Look at Shakespeare, Bacon, and Milton; were these your pure imagination men? The least of them, whichever it was, carried a jewel of poetry about him worth all his tribe that came after." It is easy to transfer this dictum to our Art. Those who, on the one hand, think Bach a dry, mathematical music constructor, without imagination or poetry; or, on the other hand, think—if, indeed, *think* is not too lofty a word—but who say or imply, that Mozart and Haydn were pretty, indeed, melodious, but slight, jejeune, not to be compared with,—well, I need mention no incomparable names; such, I submit, are not "all-round" artists; they lack perspective, they lack just what they pride themselves upon—breadth; they do not comprehend Art in its essence. It is almost amusing to hear such so-called, self-considered artists, self-complacently profess that Beethoven is their *beau-ideal*, that he only, or with such as have carried on his work, forsooth, satisfies their capacious, soaring spirits; and that to *interpret*—that is the slang-phrase—the creations of this great *tone-poet*—another slang-phrase—is their mission! They are up to him; Mozart is not up to them! Well-a-day!

Little children like to play at being kings and queens. But then *little* children grow into sensible men and women. But there are *overgrown* children, hoydens ; these have done growing; they may puff out, they do not become better proportioned.

Of such all-round men as I have spoken of, there are not very many; of half-trained men, plenty. If, because of this plenteousness, however, young aspirants complain that the profession is overstocked, one can but say, with the American lawyer, "There is plenty of room up at the top."

We occupy, then, the position of representatives, upholders, exponents, and teachers, of the Art which gives its name to our profession, *Music.* We have our specialities ; one is a vocalist, or teacher of singing ; another is a pianist ; another a theorist, or a composer; another combines two or more branches ; but our Art is *Music.* We may, indeed, speak of the art of singing, the art of composition, and so forth ; but, in the phrase "*Our Art and our Profession,*" I contemplate our Profession as *Musicians* first, as pianists, vocalists, and the like, subordinately, or merely because there must be limitation. When one writer said, "The art of singing is the same on all instruments," he gave utterance to a wider truth than the words themselves might seem to express. Our Art is the expression of the beautiful, the proportioned, the emotional, the impassioned, the ideal, the perfect,—ah ! words fail me to tell what it expresses. But this, the pure, the lovely, the exquisite, the yearning, the sublime; this, all this, and more, is our Art; into this we profess to have gained some insight. We say that Music *is* all this, whatever be the instrumentality, voice, pipe, string, used in its production. And this we have unceasingly to illustrate and to urge, among those whom in our profession we are called to influence. We are apostles of ethereal beauty, structural symmetry, expressional purity, executive perfectness, as illustrated and exemplified in music. This is our cult. I know, indeed, full well, that certain forms of gross moral debasement may co-exist with much intellectual culture and refinement. Such is the dastard inconsistency of our poor human nature. But it *is* an inconsistency; let us keep that in mind. Though Art will not renew a corrupt soul, it is a standing protest against corruption. I know a good man who holds that it is impossible to commit a bad act while beholding a beautiful flower. It ought to be so. I well remember how, as a youth, when my own impressionableness was opening up to the meaning of Mozart's and Beethoven's Sonatas, my feeling was, —how could one go and do any thing base after hearing such music! And however fallacious such a feeling may unhappily prove to be, after the rougher experiences of actual life, yet the feeling was a true one, a healthy one; and it is this sort of feeling about our Art which we have to cherish in ourselves and in our pupils, and in any public that we can influence. A pupil of mine, playing an Adagio of Beethoven's to me, having difficulty with a passage, was irritated into a petulant, impatient, expletive. I simply said—"Hush! you must not say that, while engaged with such a movement as this;"—even as I should have rebuked any one for keeping on his hat in a cathedral: it is sacrilege.

And if this be so, how petty all professional squabbles, feuds, jealousies! how vile all pandering to low tastes in production or performance!—when we represent so beautiful an Art.

Ethereal as our Art is, it has none of the lightness or evanescence of ether. It has resources for satisfying the most rigid exactions of logical acumen, or mathematical accuracy. I cannot well think any higher mental achievement possible, any greater intellectual strength attainable, than is exemplified in Bach's Art of Fugue, with its wellnigh incredible contrapuntal involvements, Fugues taken, *en masse*, by inverse movement, and the like. We must rise to the dignity of our Art if we cannot attain to all its power, or emulate the achievements of the giants of those days. "Those days"; for if we of the nineteenth century were not so puffed up with the notion of belonging to an "advanced" school, we should acknowledge that we are but as grasshoppers; we pigmies before those Anakim!

> *Of all the lamentable debts incurred*
> *By man through buying knowledge, this were worst:*
> *That he should find his last gain prove his first*
> *Was futile.**

But at least let us, now and then, try to instil some perception of the severer characteristics of our Art; so that, while I know even an intelligent man who cannot understand how there can be anything of the nature of *science*, that is, philosophy, ratiocination, and the like, about Music, we shall, as occasion presents, shew that it can hold its own in the presence of thinkers, however lofty, however profound.

For truly we have only, as professors, to be up to the level of our Art, to hold our own with culture of any kind or degree. Whether we consider Literature, Art, or Science, *our* Art has the analogue to whatever they can furnish. I say "*our* Art" as I say "*our* Profession." It is curious, and I have never heard it accounted for, that those who practise one art—the pictorial—should be so generally designated by distinction as *artists*; so that to say that a man is an artist is understood to mean that he is,—not a sculptor, not an engraver, not a musician, but a painter. Be that as it may, I speak not of Art in the abstract, nor of the departments or phases of Art, nor of the art of doing something, playing the pianoforte, or the

---

* Browning's *Parleyings*, p. 213.

like, but of *our* Art, which is special, and stands alone,—I do not say higher, nor certainly lower than other arts, but alone. It is not a representative, or imitative, or selective art; it simply has its own function, which is unique and inimitable, not very definable. It has to do, like all fine art, with the beautiful, the pure, the sublime, the perfect, the yearning; it not only has to do with it, not only expresses it, but it creates it. And not only has it this function, but it links itself also with other faculties of the mind than the imaginative or the observant; it is ratiocinative, logical, structural, and coherent. And just as the union of the imaginative with the scientific spirit is that which has suggested discovery and prompted experiment, so in Musical Composition. Instinct of something beyond, with competent knowledge and capacity to essay, these have enlarged the boundaries of our Art, as of science and art generally. Jean Mouton, Claudio Monteverde, Johann Sebastian Bach, Beethoven, and others, have been artistic innovators and discoverers in this way.

Music seems to me to have such intimate affinities with all that should occupy the intellect, fire the imagination, kindle the emotions, awaken the sympathies, appeal to the taste, that I feel that it is not only, as Shakespeare says, that

Music and sweet poetry agree,
As they must needs, the sister and the brother,

but that Music is all-embracing; and therefore the taste and the culture of Professors of Music should be wide and sympathetic. We have suffered in our own minds and characters, as well as in our social *status*, by not being true to our Art. We have not availed ourselves of the influence of our glorious Art to sharpen our perceptions, and refine our sensibilities with regard to the beauties out of its range, nor yielded to its readiness to lead us into other regions of enjoyment. Personally, may I be allowed to say, I find myself looking at very much through a musical medium or atmosphere, which is out of the immediate domain of my Art,—your Art. Congruity, compliance with much that I know and feel about the principles of musical propriety, beauty, structure, is with me a canon of criticism, a touchstone whereby I test excellence of other kinds. I do not find myself often in the wrong in this way; and, while much enjoyment is associated with the mental habit—and, as it seems to me, some clearness of vision—I receive in the processes of thought fresh and constant approval of our Art as so sweetly reasonable and logical, as well as imaginative. But, in whatever way, we must prove our worthiness to take rank with cultured thinkers by thus allying ourselves with our Art in all its refining and ennobling tendencies. We are associated as "professional musicians"; that is, as those whose *calling* is *Music*, who profess that, with all that it involves of responsibility to be consistently cultured, refined, noble. We are not pundits; we are not esoteric in our profession. But that which is our business pursuit we profess to have entered into as the realm of our intellectual enjoyment, enrichment, and culture.

There is abundant scope for the employment of every order of mind among us. For the antiquarian and historical there is a rich field, not in the compiling of chronological tables and such matters—useful, necessary work as that may be—but in tracing the historical development of our Art; not the vicissitudes and vagaries of popular taste, but the artistic researches and growths of earnest musical minds, and the formation of musical idioms, the mutations of tonalities, the gradual and progressive application of technical resources and theoretical methods to the development of musical ideas;—all this and much more, which, however, it must be admitted, requires that luxury of which we have so little—learned leisure. But it is a most interesting pursuit. Changing the field for another order of mind, there is that habit of tracing analogies between literary or other artistic forms and methods and those of our Art, lyrical or epic, narrative or dialectic, descriptive (not imitational) or speculative. I might go on with the enumeration. But the point is this. Men of culture who love Music as a sentient and intellectual enjoyment, but who are not furnished as musicians theoretically—those whom we call *amateurs*—do more or less pursue these lines of thought, and, by reason of their mental training, pursue them with more of disciplined and varied assiduity than some of ourselves, and therefore know and perceive more about the relations and some of the powers of our Art than we do. Instead of any professional cynicism at the "amateurishness" which often characterises the doings and sayings of these, and especially marks their practical musical doings, let us rather emulate their general intelligence, and so supplement and consolidate our special technical theoretical training and practical knowledge. And let it be felt by ourselves, exemplified in our doings, and understood by outsiders, that we are banded together as a Society of Professional Musicians, not for defence against assaults of other cultured spirits, but to strengthen one another to become and to illustrate what is involved in bearing, professionally and worthily, the honoured name, which may and should compass so much of erudition, cultivation, grace, and attainment,—MUSICIANS.

II

Some Methods of Musical Study

[*Read before the North-East London Society of Musicians,
December* 21st, 1886]

Some Methods of Musical Study.

My first words to you must be of congratulation, and of thanks, appreciative thanks, for the honour that you have done me in welcoming me among you, though not one of your local body. I congratulate the members of the North-East London Society of Musicians on the spirit shewn in thus associating to quicken and cement one another's interest in the pure and lovely Art. If Charles Kingsley is right in apostrophising the North-East Wind as that which, with its

Hard grey weather
Breeds hard English men,

and as

Strong within us
Bracing brain and sinew,—

then I may assume that you, in this North-East region, have experienced some of this brain-bracing, and have felt that you have mental and musical sinew enough to warrant your thus establishing yourselves in musical conclave. And, as your visitor from the not very enervating North-West, and therefore, your neighbour, and, moreover, as one with you in devotedness to all that concerns music in its strength and purity, I can only, first of all say, Go on and prosper. You have asked me to say more, however.

The suggestion was made to me by my very old professional friend, your excellent Vice-President, Dr. Monk, that a short paper, out of my own experience, on the best methods of study, either in harmony or practical music, would do well for me to read to you this evening. I half assented to his suggestion, partly, I must own, because it saved me from casting about for a subject. Moreover, it would be affectation for me to disclaim all qualification or preparation for some treatment of this subject. Having been a student of music all my life, since the period when study was possible, and a professor, trying to help others, for a period of nearly forty years, I must indeed be singularly unsympathetic, remarkably unreflective and unobservant, and perversely unwilling to profit by my opportunities, if I am not able to offer some advice, to throw out some hints, which may be adapted to be helpful to those who are still struggling as I have struggled, endeavouring as I have endeavoured, studying as I am still studying. For, believe me, I am your fellow-student; not your pedagogue. I I would not come here at all, at least, I would not speak to you on such a subject as that which I have in hand, if I were supposed to be speaking *ex cathedrâ*. I shall certainly not dogmatise. And I do not wish to be at all polemical, for, though a lover of nature, there is one object in nature which I have no liking for, that is a hornet's nest.

I have spoken of those who are "endeavouring as I have endeavoured." For, be it remembered, *study* is more than, is not identical with, *learning*, it is *endeavour*. In this sense the Apostle Paul uses the word when he enjoins upon those to whom he writes that they "*study* to be quiet." That is not the acquisition of knowledge, but the direction of the thoughts and the efforts to a certain end. And so Milton speaks of some—

> *By their guise*
> *Just men they seemed, and all their study bent*
> *To worship God aright, and know His works*
> *Not hid.**

In other words, I speak to those who study with a purpose; though the very expression is redundant. But Lord Bacon says that "Studies serve for delight, for ornament, and for ability." And I will assume that, in various degrees and proportions, these ends are your endeavour, and that it is with this present to my mind that I am to address you on Methods of Musical Study. And therefore, I feel sure that none of you who have thought it worth your while to come here will expostulate with me as having to quote Shakespeare—

---

* *Paradise Lost*, bk. xi. l. 576, etc.

> *Never read so far*
> *To know the cause why music was ordained!*
> *Was it not, to refresh the mind of man,*
> *After his studies, or his usual pain.**

"For," as Ben Jonson says, and it surely applies in an eminent degree to this our study, "Change is a kind of refreshing in studies, and infuseth knowledge by way of recreation."

Remember, then, that it is *music* that we study, and not books about music, or theories of music, except so far as they help us in the endeavour to assimilate music with our being. That is our aim, not the knowing a number of facts, nor a series of rules.

You must not expect then, that I am about to discuss Methods of Musical Study by entering on any such "kittle questions" as "Tonic Sol-fa" *v.* "Fixed Do," or the "Cramer, Potter and Bennett manner of Pianoforte playing and practice" *v.* "Higher development," or "Old School" *v.* "Harrow School," or " Double-rooted chords " *v.* "Chromatic alterations." In all these matters, after all, musical students are largely the creatures, I must not say *victims*, of circumstance, and pursue the course advised by their teachers—with whose province I *will* not interfere—or necessitated by prospective examinations, with the requirements of which I *cannot* interfere. We have to do with a beautiful Art, nay, to fascinate us yet more, we may feel

---

* *Taming of the Shrew*, Act III., Scene 1.

that we are wooing the "heavenly maid" who is ever "young"; and who, like every other sweet genuine maiden yields no charm save to unfeigned and ardent devotedness. Therefore I urge that, with whatever industry and application we may study theories of music, and compare rival theories even, we must take care that we study music itself; and, I would even say, that, while we do this, we should deduce our theories from the music that we study, rather than bring our theories as the touchstone to the music, to test its quality. At all events, let not any of our theoretical studies or notions be suffered to interfere with our unsophisticated enjoyment of, and our unfettered attachment to, music itself. In this, at least, let it be that whatever study there may be "for ability," as Lord Bacon puts it, we shall never neglect or suffer to become subordinate, the study "for delight." If I put this in another way, it would be in the way of entreaty to professional students never to let the perfecting of their qualifications for the exercise of their craft operate in any way to dull their spontaneous delight in that which they are pursuing.

But now, when I urge that we study music rather than, or in addition to, and in conjunction with, books about music, I of course mean musical compositions of that highest class which, by reason of its highest class, is designated *Classical*. And here let me take the opportunity of rebutting the charge of pedantry, bigotry, and the like, which is sometimes brought, or at least implied, against those who, like myself, counsel the study of the *Classical* models, in preference to the music of the so-called *Romantic* school. Nay, I will bring the matter to a very narrow issue by saying at once, in the most undisguised, unreserved way,—study *only* the *Classical*. Of course I shall arouse at once the exclamation, " Well, that is the veriest old-fashioned prejudice of the narrowest type; the which, if it were followed, and had been followed all along, would have retarded all progress and petrified the art." But, I reply, stay awhile. I have said nothing that tends in any such direction. I would say, in the most frank and unreserved manner, open your minds to all new impressions, receive with welcome and avidity all that bears evidence of enthusiasm, inspiration, earnestness, romanticism, if you will. Never ally yourselves with any narrow discipleship which would say to any earnest artistic producer or school of producers, " We forbid him, because he followeth not us." But I have counselled study of *Classical* models as distinguished from music of the *Romantic* school, as it is termed, because, as it seems to me, that is, in the nature of the case, the only music that can yield profit to the student; nay, more, the only music that can be *structurally* studied. Without attempting just now to define the two schools, I may succinctly, for convenience, speak of the *Classical* as *structural* music, the *Romantic* as *effluent, emotional.* Only, be it enunciated most emphatically that, while the Classical school repudiates any sense of trammeldom in being structural, the Romantic school avowedly abandons itself to unfettered—I must not say disorderly, but may say, perhaps, experimental or empirical—imaginativeness. And this very avowal, as it seems to me, while it by no means implies any lack of beauty—nay, even renders the music so wrought psychologically most interesting—nevertheless removes it from the domain of studiable music, however enjoyable. Whereas that which is structural, into which plan, design, logic, rhetoric, all enter to produce a work not of feeling and imagination and emotion merely, but of art, invites study, examination, contemplation; and will repay it just in the proportion in which it fills its avowed purpose. A work of undisciplined and, as it is said, unfettered imagination may *touch* me, "*fetch*" me, and I may feel sympathetically how the producer felt; but I cannot go and feel likewise. But a work of structure I can so study as to understand how it was done; though, of course, if I have not the inspiring genius and the disciplined scholarship, I may equally despair of ever going and doing likewise.

Take, for example, such compositions as the Sonatas of Weber, which I have enjoyed for their genius and outbursting as much as any one. They are the offspring of an eminently romantic mind, and they are certainly cast in a classical mould. But they yield little or nothing to the student of structure; there is small amount of real unfolding of the inner richness of an idea. The ideas in them are themselves almost voluptuous in their richness, but it all comes to the surface. They are not analysable as models.

Moreover, if a student desires to analyse with a view to composing, it is so immensely important that he should discipline himself in regular manners of treatment and structure (such as those which sufficed for the older classics) before he tries to adopt exceptional methods, essayed occasionally by the older masters, oftener by moderns. For a student may rest assured that in these exceptional structures and exceptional progressions in harmony, that which has been a stroke of genius in the case of a master is most likely simply a blunder of inexperience in a tyro. Because even old-fashioned but always fresh Papa Haydn, in a Sonata in E flat, goes into E natural major, it does not follow that that is a proper key for any young, inexperienced, or slightly "*uppish*" writer to go into. The presumption is, if he gets there, that he has lost his way. And so with other cases.

I return then to my counsel,—study music itself. Abandon yourself to its sensuous and emotional charms; but, as you have to do with an art as well as with an effluence,—with a production of intellect, judgment, proportion, as well as of imagination,—study, analyse, reason about music by those who are acknowledged as masters as well as geniuses; those who have attained to mastery of resources, as well as expressed the depths of their own thought and feeling. These masters are our classics, or we have none; and that, none of us would contend. These Classics are to be our study. While those who produce—I might almost say *emit*—music which is the offshoot, the offspring, if you will, of imagination which boasts of being unfettered, and which sometimes is as unregulated as it is unfettered, their emotions having had free play, which is often disordered,—it may almost be said with regard to the two schools, if schools they are to be called—the Classics and the Romanticists—as was said in reply to those who sneered at Ben Jonson's dramas, plays, being collectively termed his works, "Ben's plays are works, while others' works are plays." Students are workers, and they study works. And while that which, boasting of its spontaneity, yields nothing more to renewed hearing than repetition of the same pleasure, which is sure to pall ultimately; that which has been not merely felt, but thought and wrought, will yield to the earnest student material for renewed thought, and intelligent as well as emotional and sentient enjoyment.

The terrible sensationalism which, in this our time, has become a bye-word, and which is wholly a degradation of all that it affects, has not left Music untouched. How often are the expressions now-a-days used, with regard to certain orchestral writers, "What wonderful instrumentation!" "What effects he produces!" "How he uses the brass!" and this by young people and others who are totally ignorant of the first principles of orchestration. Now, of course, instrumentation is a beautiful art, worthy of the utmost and most detailed study by all musical students. But then it is as a mode of expression that it is thus beautiful and worthy, and not for its own sensational effect. A student who intends to score for the orchestra must undoubtedly study effects, in order to present his ideas in the most appropriate and adapted manner; and by all means let him study these from any writers who produce effects. But just as language is valuable in so far as it expresses thoughts with force, clearness, and persuasiveness, and has missed its mark if it diverts attention to itself, so it betrays an unhealthy, a false view of the art, a degraded sensationalism, if that which is most prominent in, and most persistently reiterated about, any composer, is the effects he produces by his instrumentation, and that, moreover, by the wind and especially the brass. One is inclined to say with Landor, "I have always a suspicion of sonorous sentences. The full shell sounds little, but shews by that little what is within. A bladder swells out more with wind than with oil." To be effective is not the bad thing; it is the thinking about the effect rather than about the idea that implies sensationalism, either in the listener or the composer, or both.

Of course the kind of study which I am recommending is analytical study, aided by the knowledge, not of rules but of principles, and of structural methods and devices. For this is the object which should be set before students of musical grammar; which comprehensive term, embracing as it does in language—orthography, etymology, syntax and prosody, includes in music—keys and intervals, chords, part-writing, and rhythm. And when I say chords and part-writing, I might substitute the terms *harmony* and *counterpoint*. Moreover, one who wishes to study music must study more than its grammar: there is the logic and rhetoric of the language; all the resources and appliances of musical development, such as modulation, imitation, fugue, subject-working, and movement-structure.

I am almost saddened, sometimes, by the thought of how long, too long, a time is spent needlessly in the study of *harmony*, and those elements of musical grammar which inevitably precede or accompany that study; and of how needlessly repellent and perplexing it is rendered by the way in which it is approached, taught, and studied. I think it is so, partly because, in general, it seems to be assumed that the end, the goal of it all, is to *compose* music instead of to *understand* it. And partly, also, because even with regard to the exercises that students are set to work, on the assumption that writing, or at least harmonising if not composing is the end to be aimed at, so large a proportion of the directions given are *negative*, rather than *positive*; directions as to what *not* to do. It reminds me of the elder sister saying to the younger, "Polly, do go and see what baby is doing and tell him he mustn't." And students seem only too naturally to fall into the habit of regarding the study of harmony as the training to remember and observe a number of prohibitive rules. They seldom say, "I have aimed at such and such a result; is there any way in which I can still better accomplish it?"—but, they ask, "Is it wrong?" and if one is legally compelled to say "No," they seem satisfied. Positive beauty seems scarcely thought of as attainable or even desirable; perhaps because of the dryness of the exercises set them. But to return to the remark with which I set out as to the long process which the study of harmony is turned into. Sterndale Bennett used to say to me and to others, "All that is essential about harmony may be written upon a sheet of paper;" and latterly, he reduced his estimate to half a sheet. And really, how has it come to be possible that so very extended and complicated a business has been made of it? When once the elementary matters of scales, keys, and intervals have been mastered—and surely that need not take a very long time—the few chords that there are in music with their usual context and treatment can be tabulated and illustrated in, at all events, a few pages. And granting that the complications of combinations and contexts arising from suspensions and unessential notes do considerably add to the intricacies through which a student has to thread his way, yet, if the essential chords, so few, have but been clearly set forth, these additional matters after all, need not be woven into such a tangled web as to require so lengthened a drudgery to disentangle it. At all events my own growing conviction is that, keeping the training of composers out of view for a while, something like a rapid survey, a bird's-eye view of the ground, in the first instance with only such few exercises as will just fix and consolidate the knowledge so gained, would in many cases be much more satisfactory, at all events as a preliminary proceeding, than the long-drawn-out—I had almost said dreary—plodding through a host of rules positive and negative, with an equal host of exceptions, and little in the way of thread kept hold of throughout.

It is another matter, however, when we come to the study of *counterpoint.* This is essentially the composer's art, by which I do not mean that to be able to work counterpoint is to qualify as a composer; but that, without contrapuntal training a composer is as it were without sinews. Counterpoint is the composer's art, not because it supplies him with ideas, but because it suggests and trains him to use, put forth such ideas as he has with the greatest power and structural development; to make the most of his ideas.

And therefore this is no matter for rapid survey, bird's-eye view, general understanding, but for real study in the sense of endeavour. It is not something to know merely, but something to do; and emphatically something to which the old proverb, truism as it may seem, specially applies—" The way to do a thing is to do it."

Moreover, this is not a course of study to be either deferred or curtailed. Not deferred, for of all acquirable habits of mind which are to come nearest to instincts none is more important to be acquired early than the contrapuntal habit. If a flimsier or more shallow style of musical thinking has been habitual for long, it is difficult to thoroughly assume and assimilate the more sturdy and solid habit; the ratiocinative, and developing habit. The contrapuntal mood does not sit well on those who assume it late. And, still further, this habit and the skill acquired, the power attained by a contrapuntal course, need constancy and elaboration. A glimpse at the five species of simple, and the three most usual kinds of double, counterpoint will no more give aptness and power than the twice up and down the scale with five chords to follow, customarily heard from little people in schools, will give agility of finger and ease in passing the thumb under the fingers. For contrapuntal study and skill consist not in learning and remembering a series of rules. Such skill and study have to do with the art of treating a subject in a variety of ways, in varying numbers of parts, with different superpositions. The rules may serve as guards or as guides, curbing erraticism, regulating thought, and so on. But the rules, after all, are largely corrective or deterrent, not of much positive helpfulness. They neither map out a counterpoint, nor even, to any appreciative extent, suggest one. This is left to the contrivance and inventive, or at least, constructive aptitude of the worker. And the brain needs constant exercise to keep it contrapuntally pliant and expert.

And the value of this contrapuntal work lies not in the particular rules, system, method, course, entered upon or adopted. Free or strict, ancient or modern, some course of the kind is absolutely indispensable to the gaining of structural and developing power. Methods may be adapted to modern requirements, and modes of thought and treatment, or may be rigidly severe. The one or the other may be the more salutary—I waive that point for the moment. But discipline of the kind there must be. That is all that I am insisting upon.

I feel called upon, however, at this point of our discussion to say a little about the most advisable order and method of contrapuntal study. It has been the custom I suppose from time immemorial, for students to go through a course of two-part counterpoint in all five of the species first of all, then to proceed to a similar course in three parts, then in four parts, and so on. Another plan, which I have frequently adopted, is to go through each species in two parts, in three parts, and then in four parts, before proceeding to the next species in the recognised series. This is assuredly a better way. But, for long, it has been to my mind pretty evident that if two-part counterpoint is to be from any intelligence valid, it must be based upon a more or less clear understanding of what the complete harmony would be, which is to be represented or implied by the two parts. Moreover, whereas in the earlier times of modern musical study, two-part counterpoint was somewhat empirically written with little or no reference to an implied complete harmony, which indeed was not then formulated; we, in more recent times, base our counterpoint—or should do so—on a recognised set of harmonies. And the study of counterpoint is not usually begun until the learner has made some progress with the study of chords, and the working of figured-bass exercises. Therefore it has seemed to me more reasonable at least to begin the explanation of contrapuntal work by some four-part examples, not only because by this means the complete harmonies are thereby exhibited, which are afterwards reduced to three parts and then to two; but also because, by such a demonstration, the philosophy of counterpoint is illustrated, its aim being to train the student to the habit of thinking of how a subject may be treated as an upper or highest part, as a lower or lowest, and as an inner part; and thus to set before him the ultimate goal which is to induce and encourage him to pursue a contrapuntal course at all. This preparatory four-part work with the subject taken in each part successively, I have generally superintended personally; perhaps giving the student in the first instance, the *canto fermo* as an unfigured bass, then as a melody, to be worked alone; and then introducing him to the less familiar task of placing that same subject in the inner parts. I have found the plan work well. It was devised, originally, in my own teaching; but I was gratified afterwards, to find that a similar view was enunciated by Richter. And I have been still more recently further confirmed in my opinion by reading in Spitta's Life of Bach,* that the great Sebastian himself "preferred the method which leads straight on, after treating of intervals to chords, chord combinations, and modulations, and after that too, not to begin with two-part counterpoint, but with simple counterpoint in four parts." And Spitta adds, "Quite in accordance with Bach's opinion is Kirnberger's statement that it is best to begin with four-part counterpoint, because it is impossible to write good two or three-part counterpoint until one is familiar with that in four parts. For as the harmony must necessarily be incomplete, one who is not thoroughly acquainted with four-part writing cannot decide with certainty what should be left out of the harmony in any given case."

In fact, the mistake lies in making any broad line of distinction between *harmony* and *counterpoint*, as though they were sufficiently contrasted to be almost, in a sense, antagonistic. I have heard it said, "Such and such is allowed in harmony but not in counterpoint," or "So and so is forbidden in counterpoint but not in harmony." But the real truth is that all which is generally grouped together under the head of harmony and thorough-bass, on the one hand, as matter for study, and all that is called counterpoint for practice, on the other hand, in each case represents Music; but approached,

---

* Vol. III., p. 121.

considered, and studied in a different manner, a different aspect, and from a different standpoint. The course of exercises is different in the one case from the other. In *strict style* counterpoint, undoubtedly, there is a severe restrictive discipline, which does not apply in modern free harmony. But therein lies the distinction.

Without a course of contrapuntal study many points of interest in musical works will pass unheeded. Such, for example, as that No. 1 of Bach's Inventions in two parts is entirely evolved from the first bar as its protoplasm, the two figures therein contained being treated by inverse movement, by augmentation, by double counterpoint, and so on throughout, only one half-bar being independent and unsuggested by that first bar; thus shewing what richness there may be in a germ-thought, and wherein power may be manifested in two-part writing. Or again, that in the fugal chorus in *Judas Maccabæus*, "To our great God be all the honour given," the counterpoint to the subject is that subject itself slightly modified by inverse movement at a *stretto* of half a bar; and this counterpoint, being a double counterpoint, is a true counter-subject, constituting the Fugue a double Fugue, the two subjects (really one twofold subject) being presented by inversion; but whereas the *direct* subject has to be, and is, answered *tonally*, the *inverse* form of that subject, on the other hand, has a real answer. These are obvious things enough to most of my hearers, I will readily believe; and I should almost apologise for citing them before so intelligent an audience able to find them out as well as I am, but that there may be some uninitiated who are content with their uninitiation, and who at the very recounting of such a series of technicalities may almost ask, "How can these things be?" And my reply must be, that the finding out and the pondering such things is one of the most attractive of the Methods of Musical Study about which I am speaking to you. This "learned task" is not by any means to be credited with *dry-as-dustiness.*

Counterpoint was once termed by Sterndale Bennett (I think, in a Cambridge lecture) "the *gymnastics* of music"; by which doubtless he meant that kind of exercise which is adapted to impart to the musical intellect the suppleness and strength which gymnastic training imparts to the body; the capacity to accomplish any thing muscularly, on the one hand; to work subjects any way musically, on the other; but all the while ignoring any mere acrobaticism, and, moreover, remembering that the exercises in question are means to an end, not themselves that end. But at the same time there is this difference between the muscular and the mental training,—that the muscular exercises only strengthen and develop the limbs used, and shew what can be accomplished, which is, however, not of itself worth accomplishing; but the contrapuntal gymnastics not only develop the mental powers in working on a musical theme, but also develop the latent power of the theme itself, its suggestiveness and condensed meaning. It is only too true that this may and often does degenerate instead of developing, and becomes a mere bit of pedantry; but those who have never had the application to discipline themselves by such a course of study are generally the first to raise this cry of pedantry. Surely pedantry need not be narrow-mindedness; or rather, perhaps, I should say that the term is not seldom applied where pantology would be more appropriate and just. Assuredly a course of contrapuntal study tends not to narrow and circumscribe, but to enlarge the view of the well-nigh boundless structural possibilities of this most inspired and imaginative of the arts. A contrapuntally trained mind has stamina as well as impressionableness or susceptibility. There is no necessary antagonism between the two. If the one may degenerate into pedanticism, so may the other into affectation and sickly sentimentalism. It is, perhaps, less unhealthy to be over-mathematical or metaphysical than to be dithyrambic.

But, remembering Bacon's saying that "studies serve for delight," I reiterate that the capacity for appreciative enjoyment of music is greatly enlarged by such study as that which we have been considering. Walter Savage Landor says, "Good poetry, like good music, pleases most people; but the ignorant and inexpert lose half its pleasures, the invidious lose them all. What a paradise lost is here!" The inexpert in music may be considered as those who have never in any way tried to do it, *i.e.* to construct or to study construction. Such persons, in listening to music, are somewhat like those spoken of by the same writer, who "walk over the earth, and are ignorant not only what minerals lie beneath, but what herbs and foliage they are treading."

A little while ago I was in the close of a beautiful cathedral, which I had, like others, admired for its general features. But while I was resting on a stone, some men in common garb sauntering past, stopped, and began pointing out to one another the minute carvings in stone over one of the porches, being evidently amazed at its beautiful detail. I at once discerned that they were craftsmen, who were able so much better than I to appreciate the design, the patience, the labour, the skill manifest in the wrought work. And though with mere natural perception of beauty, one may enjoy sweet melody harmoniously set, and may sometimes almost incline to say to a contrapuntist, as Emerson makes an ordinary nature-lover say to the botanist

> *Go thou to thy learned task,*
> *I stay with the flowers of spring;*
> *Do thou of the ages ask*
> *What me the hours will bring—*

yet, after all, there is immense enjoyment in being in the cunning secret of how the musical composer goes to work to produce a complete and beautiful whole.

It is a pleasant association with that same cathedral of which I have spoken, that, after his visits to it, where he much enjoyed the musical service, saying that "cathedral music elevated his soul and was his heaven upon earth," pious George Herbert, before his return to his parish church at Bemerton, "would usually sing and play his part at an appointed private music meeting; and, to justify this practice, he would often say, Religion does not banish mirth, but only moderates and sets rules to it." For "his chiefest recreation was music"—(I quote from Izaak Walton)—"in which heavenly art he was a most excellent master, and did himself compose many divine hymns and anthems, which he set and sung to his lute or viol."

Yes, indeed, if musical practice and delight needed any justifying, it might well plead this,— that, with all the ecstacy of its mirth and glee (I take glee in its original sense), it has, even as religion, rules to moderate it, rules springing out of the fitness of things. And because of this it is so excellent a study. What is there which is lovely, gracious, proportioned, reasonable, which has not its counterpart in music? What rules for just and sweet conduct of life which have not their analogue in the principles which regulate musical writing and the conduct of musical ideas? There may be all the abandonment, the ecstacy, the yearning, which shall cry with the poet—

> *Let me drink of the spirit of that sweet sound,*
> *More, O more! I am thirsting yet.*
> *It loosens the serpent which care has bound*
> *Upon my heart to stifle it;*
> *The dissolving strain, through every vein,*
> *Passes into my heart and brain.**

But then, even as life itself is not yearning, longing, sentiment, idealising, hoping only, but also real thinking to a purpose, acting, doing, painstaking, planning, constructing,—so with Music. It has been described as "both sunshine and irrigation to the mind." If sunshine, it cannot be dull; if irrigation, it cannot be dry. It calls into play the severer and more exact faculties of the intellect as well as the imagination and the emotions; and thus its study may be as good a mental discipline as any other, perhaps, if thoroughly pursued to its sweet end.

---

* Shelley.

III

Some Musical Ethics and Analogies

[*Read before the College of Organists, June* 5*th*, 1883]

Some Musical Ethics and Analogies.

IN announcing as the subject of my paper "Some Musical Ethics and Analogies," I have proposed to myself some treatment of our beautiful Art other than technical; some considerations concerning it which shall be a relief from that theoretical method of speaking about it to which our professional habits render us so liable; and, moreover, some way of looking at and treatment of it which shall not lead us into the region of pure æsthetics—whatever that may be—any more than into the technical region which we know only too well. I have thought that the terms *Ethics* and *Analogies* may be sufficiently elastic to include such informal and untechnical considerations as those which I propose submitting to you.

By *Ethics* we understand, speaking generally, *moral laws;* by the ethics of any subject the moral laws affecting or exemplified by that subject. By *Analogy* we understand the *resemblances* between any two matters, or rather between their *relation-*

ships, bearings, influences, and the like.* By *Musical Ethics and Analogies*, or better still, the *Ethics and Analogies of Music*, then, it is implied that, in certain important senses, Music does not stand alone, isolated, independent; *moral considerations* affect it as they do other matters; and that, on the other hand, although it is in some respects *unique*, it has counterparts and analogies which may serve to illustrate it, clear our perceptions about it and increase our interest in it. For I have always found that my acquaintance with musical art has enhanced my enjoyment of all else that is imaginative, ideal, and artistically structural. And there may be a *vice versâ;* a reflex process.

All of you musicians are familiar enough with, and know what I mean when I talk of, the *German* 6th, the *French* 6th, the *Italian* 6th, the *Neapolitan* 6th, the *Major* and *Minor Triads*, the *Diminished Triad*, the *Augmented Triad*. I doubt however whether you will feel quite so much at home if I venture to refer to the *Welsh Triads*. Pardon me if I do you injustice; but of course you do not all come from the Principality, nor have you all been to an *Eisteddfod*. These *Welsh Triads* are, I

---

* "Analogy does not mean the similarity of two *things*, but the similarity or sameness of two *relations*. There must be more than two *things* to give rise to two relations; there must be at least three; and in most cases there are four." (Copleston's *Four Discourses*, note to Disc. iii.)

understand, a collection of poetical histories, mythologies, ethical and legal maxims, etc., tersely expressed, and all in groups of three; hence their name. Now one of these *Triads* enunciates "*the three excellencies of poetry: simplicity of language, simplicity of subject, and simplicity of invention.*" And it strikes me that musicians should be the last to decline to accept in the form of a *Triad*, and appropriate to their own Art, the terse enunciation of one of the first foundation principles of all true art. Simplicity in character and life all rightminded men approve; simplicity of purpose, manner, and speech; whether as opposed to obscurity, mystery, or to duplicity; not at all to *profundity.* For the man of true simplicity in character and life has principles so profound, so deep down, that the waves of fashion and the gusts of passion do not disturb the consistent stedfastness of his career. It is a mistake, and an offence against the morality of words, to speak of a certain sort of bad man as *deep* and *cunning.* The man of *ken*, the *knowing* man, in the right sense of the word, is really deep and profound. And yet the man with deep knowledge and profound principles and character, is, in the truest sense, superficial; that is, there is nothing that need be buried and concealed; therefore it *comes to the surface:* you see by and on the surface what there is deep down. For when we characterise a life as marked by "*simplicity and godly sincerity,*" we use two words which mean respectively, *without fold*, and *without wax*. *Duplicity*, double-foldedness, which we all abhor—in others at least—stands opposed to *simplicity;* and *sincerity* just expresses what the finest honey is; no residuum of wax; all sweet and pure.

And this simplicity is a *moral* quality; therefore it finds its place in this treatment of *ethics*. For if there is to be simplicity of language, subject, invention, there is to be of course definiteness of aim; and this must be clearly to express a pure idea. *A pure idea;* no attempt to invest the impure with interest. "To be for ever true is the science of poetry."[*] Mendelssohn detested the having to write an overture to that which he designated the "*odious play*" of "Ruy Blas." And yet quite recently in an able journal, distinguished for its high tone, it has been declared that "music is neither good nor bad, any more than poetry or eloquence, but is a method of expression which to many organisations is capable of conveying higher, more delicate, and above all, more exact meanings than any other. But it can convey any meaning, and does very often convey a sensual one."[†] That it should have been possible to write this, may well

---

[*] Hunt's *Poetry of Science*, Introd. p. 11.
[†] *Spectator*, May 12th, 1883, p. 606.

be laid to the charge of certain composers who have debased the art by vile associations. But it has yet to be proved, I venture to submit, that music can, with definiteness or otherwise, "convey a sensual meaning." More of this anon.

But "*simplicity of invention*, does it exist in music? Yes. Bach could, with the honesty and conscience which characterised the *simple-minded* man, call his two-part and three-part movements for the clavichord Inventions. Not *Transcriptions;* oh, no. Not "*Pensées fugitives*";—no. These pieces were not mere transient, unworked, unthought effervescences, or off-shoots; they were *inventions*. He *came upon* these pieces;—*discovered* them, in the *inventory* of his marvellous mind. They were his own. And there was "*simplicity of subject*"; merely a few notes,—perhaps a section of the scale. And further, "*simplicity of language*." Not indeed without *folds;* these two-part, three-part, double-contrapuntal *inventions*. But it was the *many-sidedness*, not the evasiveness of thought; *manifold* beauty, beauties to be unfolded.

For this simplicity, it is not paradoxical to assert, by no means excludes the *complex* or *complicated*. The very mention of Bach brings the two elements to one's mind; he being such an exemplification of the union of true honest simplicity with the utmost, profoundest complicatedness. It has been well said, " True simplicity does not consist in what is trite, bald, or commonplace. So far as regards the thought, it means, not what is already obvious to everybody, but what, though not obvious, is immediately recognised as soon as propounded to be true and striking. As regards the expression, it means that thoughts worth hearing are expressed in language that everyone can understand. In the first point of view it is opposed to what is abstruse; in the second to what is obscure. It is not what some men take it to mean, threadbare commonplace expressed in insipid language. . . . True simplicity is the last and most excellent grace which can belong to a speaker, and is certainly not to be attained without much effort."* And for "speaker" here one may substitute "musician," or any other productive artist. And all this agrees with the *Welsh Triad,* "simplicity of language, subject, invention."

Of course, then, no one supposes that objection is here raised to that complexity which may be inevitably associated with elaboration. It goes without saying that in a Fugue, or other developed contrapuntal work, there will be the involvements proper to such work. But, amidst all these, that which is pleaded for is simplicity in the subject, definiteness; and, above all, non-ambiguity, non-evasiveness, non-requirement of justificatory expla-

---

* *Edinburgh Review*, Oct. 1840, pp. 94—98.

nation. This is a matter which, I am persuaded from constant experience, needs impressing upon musical students and young composers just now. Students seem to be liable to two extremes of danger;—that of thinking that knowledge alone will stand them instead of genius, and that of thinking that imagination must not be curbed by pedantic rules. Some come to us to be taught with the charmingly *naïve* ingenuousness so quaintly expressed by the old poet—

> *O my dear master, cannot you (quoth I)*
> *Make me a poet? Do it if you can,*
> *And you shall see I'll quickly be a man.**

This really is hardly an exaggeration of the sanguineness of some who come expecting that, though unable to put two chords together, a few months' easy study are to thoroughly equip them for their Bachelor's degree. On the other hand, some are so impatient of restraint, or so marvellously well-read in all the exceptions to rules, and in all just possible though rare progressions, that every bar exemplifies a rarity or a licence, and, moreover, brings into play all the student's capacity for exceptional justification, often by equivocation, theoretical equivocation. All springs from the lack of simplicity,—simplicity of thought, plan, purpose, design, language or mode of expression,

---

* Michael Drayton, *Epistle to Henry Reynolds.*

the poverty or ambiguity of the thought being disguised by eccentric, unsimple presentation,—so often the refuge of poor or confused or shallow thinkers in literature and in music.

What do we mean by *Classical*, as applied to music? With what does it stand in contrast? In scholarly pursuits, of course, the term has defined application to certain languages and productions, which are in a *class* by themselves, needing no other specification. But, in modern use of the term, is not the contrast between two manners or styles of writing, the *Classical* and the *Romantic?* Speaking of the difference, with regard to literature, and with the view to enunciate that it need not be merely an essential characterisation of the Classical and Romanesque *languages* and *ages* respectively, one well endowed with the faculty to pronounce says—

> *The classical, like the heroic age,*
> *Is past; but poetry may re-assume*
> *That glorious name with Tartar and with Turk,*
> *With Goth or Arab, Sheik or Paladin,*
> *And not with Roman or with Greek alone.*
> *The name is graven on the workmanship.**

On which an eminent critic remarks: "To define for our present purpose the difference between the classical and the romantic modes of workmanship. In classical writing every idea is called up to the

---

* W. S. Landor, *Epistle to Author of "Festus."*

mind as nakedly as possible, and at the same time as distinctly; it is exhibited in white light, and left to produce its effect by its own unaided power. In romantic writing, on the other hand, all objects are exhibited as it were through a coloured and iridescent atmosphere. Round about every central idea the romantic writer summons up a cloud of accessory and subordinate ideas for the sake of enhancing its effect, if at the risk of confusing its outlines. The temper, again, of the romantic writer is one of excitement; while the temper of the classical writer is one of self-possession. No matter what the power of his subject, the classical writer does not fail to assert his mastery over it and over himself; while the romantic writer seems as though his subject were ever on the point of dazzling and carrying him away. On the one hand there is calm, on the other hand enthusiasm; the virtues of the one style are strength of grasp, with clearness and justice of presentment; the virtues of the other style are glow of spirit, with magic and richness of suggestion."*

Now if this is in the main true, and applicable with some technical deviations to musical art, it will not be difficult—nay, I fancy it will be almost inevitable—at once to associate certain modern names with the Romantic, the iridescent school,

---

* Prof. Sidney Colvin, preface to *Selections from Landor*.

the school of excitement, dazzle, enthusiasm, glow, in all of which there may be, let us remember, life, reactionary life, reaction against pedantry, stiffness, formalism, conventionalism, stagnation, and artificialism, even as was the case with the rise of the modern Romantic school of Poetry; and so far, so good. But it is of the Classical that I am speaking specially; and about this let it be repeated—

The name is graven on the workmanship.

But then that workmanship is not the idiom or manner of an age, a country; but it is the outcome of genius and of truth and beauty, which are of and for all time.

Bach, in the case supposed, does present the idea in its unadorned purity, strength, suggestiveness. It need not shrink thus to stand; it is true, suggestive, and susceptible of true harmonies. It needs no iridescence, only white light. But then follows, —not clothing to cover it, not apology to excuse it, but trial to prove it, as though it were the stern goodness of a righteous man. And like that it comes forth as gold "purified seven times"; tested by *counterpoint*, by *tonal alteration* or modification, by *inverse movement*, by *augmentation*, by *diminution*, by *modulation*, by *stretti*. Those are seven ways; but after all seven is the perfect number, and the test is perfect.

Is there not some analogy to all this, for instance,

SOME ETHICS AND ANALOGIES.

in the longest poem by Mr. Browning? Firstly, he arrests you, accosts you with—

> *Do you see this Ring?*
> *'Tis Rome-work, made to match*
> *(By Castellani's imitative craft)*
> *Etrurian circlets found, some happy morn,*
> *After a drooping April; found alive*
> *Spark-like 'mid unearthed slope-side fig-tree roots*
> *That roof old tombs at Chiusi: soft, you see,*
> *Yet crisp as jewel-cutting. There's one trick*
> *(Craftsmen instruct me), one approved device*
> *And but one, fits such slivers of pure gold*
> *As this was,—such mere oozings from the mine,*
> *Virgin as oval tawny pendent tear*
> *At bee-hive edge when ripened combs o'erflow—*
> *To bear the file's tooth and the hammer's tap:*
> *Since hammer needs must widen out the round,*
> *And file emboss it fine with lily-flowers,*
> *Ere the stuff grow a ring-thing right to wear.**

And then he describes what that "trick" is; and in this the analogy fails, by the way, for the trick is to

> *Melt up wax with honey, so to speak,*

to

> *Mingle gold with gold's alloy.*

But then, the ring presented, he goes on—"What of it?" Yes; just what the shallow, without intuitive perception, say of an unadorned plain musical subject:

---

* *The Ring and the Book.*

> *What of it?*
> *'Tis a figure, a symbol, say;*
> *A thing's sign: now for the thing signified.*
> *Do you see this square old yellow book, I toss*
> *I' the air, and catch again, and twirl about*
> *By the vellum covers,—pure crude fact*
> *Secreted from man's life when hearts beat hard,*
> *And brains, high-blooded, ticked two centuries since?"*

Then he proceeds to give the narration of the history, the germ of all, but still "crude fact." He has given the subject, the answer, the countersubject; philosophises about, hints at, suggests the possibilities, the potentialities enclosed in that history,—even as the *exposition* of a Fugue does with what the uninitiated, the unsusceptible regard as like "pure crude fact." But then after the speculations of "*half-Rome*" and "*the other half-Rome*," —just the episode that succeeds the exposition— he proceeds to give the relation of that same history in various ways, by the various characters, with various prominences, and perhaps various suppressions, even distortions; but the same history, the same subject, in various lights,—only, mark you, with a bias in every case. Now, on the other hand, when the honest musician presents an idea, a musical thought to you, he says, as it were, " Do you see this Ring?—this Book? Do you hear this subject?."

"What of it?" say you. "Well, I will shew you what of it." And then he proceeds to shew you its richness and many-sidedness; not to leave you in bewilderment; not to suppress the weak points, exaggerate the strong, distort the doubtful,—but to shew you strength and truth all round and all through.

I do not know whether this seems to you a fancifully-wrought analogy, a mere *conceit*, in the old sense of that term. But I confess again that it is because I have learned something, practically, theoretically, and by observation, of the mode of presenting, carrying out, and developing a germ-thought in music that I can, with the enhanced pleasure that I have referred to, follow a train of thought, and to some extent enter into and apprehend an artistic production in verse or prose in any art in which continuous thought and varied many-sided presentation may find its expression. It makes me feel in sympathetic brotherhood with all true human intellects.

And this varied presentation is Classical, not ornamental. It is not polish, not external chasing, however elegant, on a surface. It is not sensuous, iridescent. It is hardly rhetorical, it is logical; it is a development of innate truth. It is presentation in *white light*, according to the previously cited definition.

But be it observed, "the re-assumption of the glorious name" of Classical is of little avail unless there be the animating spirit and power. Heroic verse presupposes, necessitates, heroes and heroic deeds; or it becomes mere bombast, or schoolboy-exercise. And this re-assumption, moreover, is a different thing from, and is not to be attained by the donning of the antique garb; by prattling in bygone speech and idiom. Fascinating indeed is it to any of us who have any measure of the historical imagination to transport ourselves into old times, old scenes, old manners, old modes of thought and of expression. This is one reason why we experience such peculiar pleasure in visiting ruined abbeys, castles, and the like;—our historical imagination seems to be thereby kindled and helped. It is in proportion to the extent of this element,—is it not? —that we have the sense of the *picturesque* in a scene. It is this element in our minds in a more or less exaggerated or distorted form that has given rise, I suppose, to the—shall I say?—*fads* or *crazes* for blue china, or for so-called æsthetic furniture or dress. And is there not in our art something of an analogous kind, in the *anachronism*, artistically speaking, of writing now-a-days pieces of music in the obsolete *dance-measures?* We may build Queen Anne houses, but then we can inhabit them. But why write *Gavottes, Bourrées,* and the like, when they are not danced now? No dance-motion such as the old writers witnessed, and were at least *prompted* if not *inspired* by, now impels our writers. Manufactured picturesqueness is surely a strange fad. I know a house, by the side of a London canal, where there is a manufactured ruin of an abbey, I believe made of virgin cork, with vacant window frames and so on, on a slope down to the water's edge. I am not impressed by it, neither am I carried back to old times by a modern *Gavotte*. Does any one say, "Oh! I like the *quaintness* of it." Ah! listen to what an authority on philology says about that word *quaint*:—

"Its primary meaning is artificially [not *artistically*] elegant or ingenious, then affectedly artificial, and finally, odd, antique, yet retaining always an element of the pleasing. The idea of quaintness belongs at present most commonly to style of thought and verbal expression in which appears a combination of fancy, originality, delicacy, and force, yet a disharmony with present modes. Quaint architecture, for instance, is in detail antiquated and curious, shewing an obsolete beauty and an unfashionable ingenuity."*

Now rest assured, I make no personal allusions, and have not any personal references in my mind. I freely acknowledge the charm of some modern movements of this class that I have heard, and I know what a pleasurable pastime it is, in one's lighter moments, to exercise one's fancy and ingenuity in writing such pieces. I only would,

---

* Archdeacon C. J. Smith, *Synonyms Discriminated.*

with all kindness, caution young writers against throwing dust into their own eyes by disguising perhaps very ordinary thoughts in this quaint garb. "*Quaint*" and, as Sterndale Bennett used to say to me, "*characteristic*" are rather dangerous words.

These attempts to reproduce old manners are not often successful. Even so great a man as Spohr, in his *historical symphony*, is generally considered not to have *reproduced* anything from Handel to Auber, but to have re-illustrated his own versatility in conjunction with his *mannerism;* the movements after all only represent Spohr in different suits of clothes. Those of us who remember the *man*, know very well that Mozart's clothes would have been a misfit; and so with Mozart's *style*, that would not fit the *musician* Spohr.

There are many other analogies and ethics to which I might draw your attention, but time warns me that I must hardly even venture upon the summing-up of what I have, as it may seem to you, somewhat discursively advanced.

What is idealising? Is it not the elimination from the object presented of all that is unbeautiful, unattractive, seizing hold of and presenting all in it that is admirable, and moreover, the discernment and making evident of all the potentialities of good, the latent beauty, pruned of that which is accidental and of the nature of excrescence; and so presenting not a false, not a distorted, not an exaggerated, not even a one-sided view, but the view of the rich possibilities, rather than the actual; because the blemishes in the actual are *from outside;* the beautiful, the good, is *from within?* Is not this what we mean by an idealised portrait? Is it not the kind of portrait that we should like our friends to take of us, of our characters?—and which it would be better for our charity to take of our friends.

Now music is not an *idealising* art; it is itself not a selective, nor an eliminatory art; it is itself in its essence, ideal. It is a *yearning* art; actually expressive of the *sensual* it *cannot* be. Music is a *sentient* art; it appeals to us through one of our senses; but *sensual* it is not. It may be that certain composers have presented it in highly-wrought *sensuous* fashion, and we are *sentient* beings. It may be that, as I said before, some have associated music with sensual surroundings. But are we to say, with the writer that I referred to, that "Music is neither good nor bad"? Because "out of the same mouth proceedeth blessing and cursing," is *language* the less a *Divine gift,* a good, therefore? And so, music is good,—a Divine gift and endowment.* That patriarch who to so many of you is

---

* "There is this peculiar advantage about melody, that *per se*, it is absolutely pure and remote from trivial ideas. The song and the dance may have their associations, good or evil, but the pure melody

only a name, but to those of us who knew him, a name always pronounced with reverence—Cipriani Potter—used to say to me—"All good music is melancholy." I fancy that what he really meant was that it is ideal. And inasmuch as the ideal is not realised, is not the actual, the real,—but the ideal still,—there will be associated with it that kind of undefined melancholy, that sense of something that might have been but is not, that wistfulness which the Laureate expresses in asking

> *Who can tell*
> *Why to smell*
> *The violet*
> *Recalls the dewy prime*
> *Of youth and buried time?*

Yes; and anything which does this,—engenders at once the dissatisfaction and the yearning, in this grovelling, sensuous, nay, sensual world,—is so far purifying. Only it is *music*, true music that must do this. After *that*, if we have ears to hear, do we not feel that which another poet has expressed only with mythological phraseology?—(we can substitute Beethoven or Handel for Apollo)—

---

in itself is pure indeed; it is gay, or pathetic, or stately or sublime, but in any case there is something in the thrill of a choice chord, and the progression of a perfect melody, which seems to raise the hearer above the trifling affairs of life. At times it 'brings all Heaven before our eyes.' . . . . Music is naturally more pure and removed from the concrete and sensuous ideas of ordinary life than a drama can usually be."—Prof. W. Stanley Jevons' *Methods of Social Reform*, pp. 9, 11.

> Oh, ecstacy!
> Oh, happiness of him who once has heard
> Apollo singing! For his ears the sound
> Of grosser music dies, and all the earth
> Is full of subtle undertones, which change
> The listener and transform him. As he sang—
> Of what I know not, but the music touched
> Each chord of being—I felt my secret life
> Stand open to it, as the parched earth yawns
> To drink the Summer rain; and at the call
> Of those refreshing waters, all my thought
> Stir from its dark and secret depths, and burst
> Into sweet odorous flowers, and from their wells
> Deep call to deep, and all the mystery
> Of all that is, laid open.*

And again the same poet, of the vocation of poet, artist, or musician :—

> To be fulfilled with Godhead as a cup
> Filled with a precious essence, till the hand,
> On marble or on canvas falling, leaves
> Celestial traces, or from reed or string
> Draws out faint echoes of the voice Divine
> That bring God nearer to a faithless world.
> Or, higher still and fairer and more blest,
> To be His seer, His prophet; to be the voice
> Of the Ineffable Word; to be the glass
> Of the Ineffable Light, and bring them down
> To bless the earth, set in a Shrine of Song.

---

* *Epic of Hades*, p. 90.

For EU product safety concerns, contact us at Calle de José Abascal, 56–1°, 28003 Madrid, Spain or eugpsr@cambridge.org.

www.ingramcontent.com/pod-product-compliance
Ingram Content Group UK Ltd.
Pitfield, Milton Keynes, MK11 3LW, UK
UKHW041421180426
11947UKWH00007B/229